MW00913863

THE
ONE THING

31-Day Devotional

JOSEPH PRINCE

The One Thing

ISBN 981-05-3541-4
© Copyright Joseph Prince, 2007

Joseph Prince Teaching Resources
www.josephprince.com

Printed in the U.S.A.
Third edition, first print: June 2014

Foreword

by Pastor Joseph Prince

Welcome to the family of God! There are probably 1,001 things competing for your attention every day. So what should your focus be? Well, Jesus gives us the answer in the Bible.

In Luke 10:38–42, when He entered the house of two sisters, one of them, Mary, sat at His feet and listened to Him. The other, Martha, rushed to the kitchen and began cooking for Him. Guess who Jesus praised?

He praised Mary.

It might surprise you that Jesus didn't praise Martha for serving and cooking for Him. Instead, He praised Mary because she focused on doing the one thing needful. So all you have to do is that one thing and God will take care of everything in your life, both big and small.

This 31-day devotional has been specially put together to help you do that one thing — to feed on Jesus' Word and be strong. It will help you build a firm foundation for your new life as a Christian. You will discover how to live a life worth living — an abundant, blessed, fulfilling, stress-free and victorious life!

The Bible says that your future is as bright as the promises of God and God never breaks His promises! So you can look forward to better days ahead because God loves you and He wants you to have good success in every area of your life.

Does that get you excited?

Then let's get started!

6 "Are not five sparrows sold for two copper coins? And not one of them is forgotten before God. 7But the very hairs of your head are all numbered. Do not fear therefore; you are of more value than many sparrows.

Luke 12:6–7

If It Matters To You, It Matters To God

Many Christians make the mistake of thinking that God is too busy taking care of the "big things" to be interested in the little problems they are facing. Are you one of them? It may be your child's bed-wetting habit, a quarrel with a friend or the small pimple on your face. No matter how trivial it sounds, if it troubles you, then God wants to take care of it!

God wants to take care of every area of your life, even the smallest detail. He loves you so much that He knows the number of hairs you have on your head. And if your loving heavenly Father knows and is interested in the small details of your life, then you don't have to overcome any problem on your own.

When my daughter Jessica turned three, my wife Wendy and I decided to bring her to Disneyland. Knowing that it was her first encounter with Disneyland and that she could be frightened by unexpected shocks, I decided to watch one of the theatre productions which I had planned to bring her to, before I took her to watch it.

As I sat through the production, my mind was on Jessica all the time. I was thinking, "Is this too frightening for her? Will she like the mechanical singing bear? Is the place too dark for her?" I decided to bring her to the show only after I had seen it myself and was sure that she would enjoy it.

My friend, your heavenly Father cares for you in the same way as He lays out His plans for you. You are on His heart all the time as He carefully considers and makes plans for every aspect of your life, both big and small. And the very thought of you puts a smile on His face because He knows that the plans He has for you are plans to bless you. (Jeremiah 29:11)

So no matter what problems you are facing right now, you can rest in His love for you. There is no problem that is too insignificant for Him to handle. He is not just God Almighty, He is also your heavenly Father who loves you!

¹He who dwells in the secret place of the Most High shall abide under the shadow of the Almighty. ²I will say of the Lord, "He is my refuge and my fortress; my God, in Him I will trust."

Psalm 91:1–2

The Lord Is Your Refuge

Every day, we are bombarded with news of conflicts, natural disasters, diseases and new strains of drug-resistant viruses. We also hear of people losing their loved ones in freak accidents. And we ask ourselves, "Is there a place where I can take refuge from a world gone mad?"

Yes, there is! God foresaw all these things and He has promised in His Word protection from every evil known to man. There is no trap set by the devil that our Father cannot deliver us from, if we trust in Him and take Him as our refuge. That is His promise in Psalm 91.

Whether it is an earthquake at midnight, a crazy sniper, an unknown virus or a terrorist attack, God says, "You shall not be afraid of the terror by night, nor of the arrow that flies by day, nor of the pestilence that walks in darkness, nor of the destruction that lays waste at noonday." (Psalm 91:5–6)

Because you have made Him your dwelling place, angels are watching over you right now. (Psalm 91:9–11) They give heed to the voice of God's Word, so you should give voice to God's Word. This means that you should agree with and speak what God's Word says about His preserving and protecting you. Then, angels are sent to minister for you. (Hebrews 1:14)

My friend, don't say, "If it can happen to them, it can also happen to me!" Say, "A thousand may fall at my side and 10,000 at my right hand, but it will not come near me!" (Psalm 91:7) The world says that you cannot but expect danger all around. God says, "You are in this world but not of this world. You have My protection because you are of Me and in Me." (John 17:14–23)

You have access by faith into the secret place of the Most High where no evil can touch you. There is no need to fear living in the end times because the Lord is your refuge and fortress. His Word says so. And those who trust His Word completely find His Word completely true!

26Look at the birds of the air, for they neither sow nor reap nor gather into barns; yet your heavenly Father feeds them. Are you not of more value than they?

Matthew 6:26

The Good Life Without The Sweat

Most people are of the opinion that the good life does not happen without hard work and buckets of sweat. They believe that to achieve success, you first need to have this educational certificate, that professional qualification, this particular job and that many years of hard work. I have good news for you: God has a better way.

We all must work, but the world wants you to believe that there is a natural process of sowing, reaping and gathering, accompanied by waiting, toiling and stress, before the good life actually comes. But God says, "My people do not need to go through this natural process to enjoy the good life for they are not of this world's system. They can operate out of My economy and I can give them the good life straightaway!"

In the same way that God feeds the birds which do not go through the sow-then-reap-then-gather system of the world, He wants to and will do much more for you!

Your heavenly Father wants you to know the generosity of His heart toward you and how much

He wants to make you successful. A case in point is what happened to a church member who believed this truth. After leaving his previous job, he trusted God to provide him with a better one. Within just four months, he found himself heading two companies.

His newly formed distribution company not only clinched a major project in Singapore, but was also made the principal distributor in Southeast Asia for a popular line of products from the United States. His second company, which provided consultancy services, was given two projects by a Korean and a Hong Kong company for a six-figure consultancy fee in US dollars.

Today, God wants you to know that you are not of the world's system. You are of the kingdom of God — the same kingdom that feeds the birds that do not toil, but simply trust their Creator for all their provisions in life. Be convinced that you are of more value to your heavenly Father than the birds, and let Him give you the good life without the toiling and laboring of the world.

[12]*But this Man, after He had offered one sacrifice for sins forever, sat down on the right hand of God...* [14]*For by one offering He hath perfected forever them that are sanctified.*

Hebrews 10:12, 14, KJV

You Are Perfect In God's Eyes

God sees you with no flaw, spot or imperfection, so honor His Word and the finished work of His Son by saying, "Amen!" Don't doubt your perfection in Christ.

To see yourself as far from being perfect is not modesty, but a failure to understand the perfect sacrifice that Jesus has made for you.

The Bible tells us, "For by one offering He hath **perfected forever** them that **are sanctified**". Did you get that? You have not only been sanctified, that is, made holy, but by the same offering of His body, you have been perfected. You are both holy and perfect in God's eyes!

Your sins have been purged perfectly. Today, Jesus is seated at His Father's right hand not because He is the Son of God (although that is true), but because His work of purging your sins is completely finished and perfect!

So instead of being conscious of your sins, which is to have an evil conscience (Hebrews 10:22), you can have a perfect conscience, a conscience that is free from the guilt and condemnation of sins.

When you find yourself conscious of your sins, just say, "Thank You, Lord Jesus, for Your wonderful work at the cross. It is a perfect work that has removed all my sins completely.

"Holy Spirit, thank You for convicting me of righteousness, not my own, but God's righteousness given to me as a gift. Keep on convicting me in the days to come, reminding me especially when I fail that I am still the righteousness of God in Christ."

My friend, God sees you perfect without any spot of sin. He sees you covered in the beautiful white robes of His own righteousness. He treats you like a righteous man because that is what He has made you. So expect good things to happen to you because blessings are on the head of the righteous! (Proverbs 10:6)

Choose Not To Worry

Many Christians are familiar with Jesus' rhetorical question, "Which of you by worrying can add one cubit to his stature?" But not many of us actually let it get into our hearts and allow the love of God to free us from our habit of worrying.

The truth is, no amount of worrying can lengthen your life or add anything to your physical person. Instead, worrying robs you of sleep, health and many good years. In fact, it is only when you are worry-free that God's anointing flows freely in you, strengthening, healing, restoring and adding to you.

A church member, after undergoing a mammogram, found that she had lumps in her breast. Upon receiving the doctor's report, she wrote this down on the report: "Jesus is my healer. I receive my healing. I am healed. I rest in God completely."

She was due back at the clinic later the same day for a biopsy to see if the lumps were malignant. Her sister-in-law, who was having lunch with her that day, witnessed her cheerful and worry-free attitude while she ate her lunch.

Back at the clinic, this precious sister sat among other ladies who were also there for their biopsies. They looked very worried, so she started sharing Jesus with them and prayed for some of them. When her turn came and she had an ultrasound scan done, the doctor was puzzled — her scan showed no evidence of any lumps!

The doctor went back to consult her colleague who had first discovered the lumps. Stunned, both doctors conducted their own investigations. They returned to her only to say, "It's a miracle!"

My friend, when you worry, you are actually believing that the devil has the power to make inroads into your life that God cannot protect you from. But when you refuse to worry, you are putting your faith in God. You have more confidence in His love and power working for you than in the devil's ability to harm you! When you refuse to worry, but choose to rest in the finished work of Christ, you will see the manifestation of your blessing. You will see your miracle!

30So when Jesus had received the sour wine, He said, "It is finished!" And bowing His head, He gave up His spirit.

John 19:30

It Is Finished!

Imagine looking at Leonardo da Vinci's famous Mona Lisa painting in the Louvre museum. Would you think of adding more brush strokes to it? Of course not! It was done by a master, so what could you possibly add to the painting to improve it?

In the same way, that is how we are to look at Jesus' work on the cross. He cried out, "It is finished!" You cannot complete a completed work. You cannot finish a finished work. Our salvation is won. Our sins are all forgiven. We are made forever righteous by His blood. Christ paid completely and perfectly for our total forgiveness, righteousness and every blessing!

In fact, these three words, "It is finished", come from one Greek word *teleo*. In the days of Jesus, a servant would use it when reporting to his master: "I have completed the work assigned to me." (John 17:4) The word means, "It is finished, it stands finished and it will always be finished!" Perhaps the most significant meaning of *teleo* is how it is used by merchants: "The debt is paid in full!" When Jesus gave Himself on the cross, He met fully the righteous demands of the law. He paid our debts in full!

Today, it is not our works that will bring us the blessings. It is Christ's finished work. Christian living is not about **doing**, but **believing** in His finished work. Under the law, we must **do**. Under grace, it is **done**!

Maybe you are faced with overwhelming odds today. Jesus promises, "It is finished!" You are not going to be delivered because you have already been delivered. You are not going to be healed because you are already the healed! God healed you 2,000 years ago! Isaiah 53:5 declares, "By His stripes you **are** healed!" You are already pregnant with healing. Keep resting in His finished work and it will manifest!

My friend, the work is finished. The victory is won. Our blessings have been bought by His blood! Live life knowing that there is nothing for you to do — only **believe**! It is finished!

Day 7

13I have given you a land for which you did not labor, and cities which you did not build, and you dwell in them; you eat of the vineyards and olive groves which you did not plant.'

Joshua 24:13

You Are Already Blessed

God is more willing to bless you than you are willing to be blessed! In fact, He is so keen for you to enjoy His abundance that in His mind, giving you over and above what you need is a settled matter.

God has already promised: "I **have given** you a land for which you did not labor, and cities which you did not build, and you dwell in them; you eat of the vineyards and olive groves which you did not plant."

He did not say, "I may give," which means that it may or may not happen, but He said, "I have given," which means that it has already happened. It is only a matter of time before your revelation of what you have through the work of Christ brings forth the abundance that He has already blessed you with.

A brother in the United States wrote in to share how he needed to buy a car, but had only half the amount of money needed. He kept calculating and strategizing, but the sums just weren't adding up. He finally quit trying to make it happen and just rested in the Lord's love and ability to provide for him. Weeks later, he was able to buy a car that was two years newer than what he had wanted, at exactly the amount that he had!

My friend, expect divine provision in your life because you are already richly blessed in Christ. Jesus took your place of poverty at the cross — "For you know the grace of our Lord Jesus Christ, that though He was rich, yet for your sakes He became poor, that you through His poverty might become rich." (2 Corinthians 8:9) In Him, you are poor no more.

So stop looking at the lack in your natural resources. Look to the cross and say, "Because of Jesus' finished work, I can expect to walk in all of His blessings!"

Day 8

³Then Jesus put out His hand and touched him, saying, "I am willing; be cleansed."…

Matthew 8:3

Jesus Is Willing, Be Healed!

Do you know that it is God's will for you to be healed? In fact, Jesus always healed the sick who came to Him. The blind, lame, maimed, mute, deaf and demon-possessed — He healed them **all**! (Matthew 8:16)

The Bible says that he who has seen Jesus has seen the Father. (John 14:9) You want to see what God is like? Look at Jesus! He never gave sickness to anybody. You never find Jesus looking at a person, a fine specimen of a man, and saying, "Come here. You are too healthy. Receive some leprosy!" In fact, when a leper came to Him for healing, Jesus, full of compassion, told the leper, "I am willing; be cleansed."

Unfortunately, there are some Christians who say, "It is God's will for me to be sick. God has some purpose, some mysterious purpose for my situation. It is all part of His divine plan and we shall all know in the sweet by and by, the reason why!" But these same people go to their doctors to get well. They take their medication and rest. Why do they do that if they really believe that God wants them sick? Doesn't make sense, does it?

Come on, what makes perfect sense is this: God wants you well. He wants you whole. His will is for you to be healed! In fact, He is so willing that He took **all** your sicknesses and diseases upon His own body, so that you don't have to suffer them today! He allowed Himself to be beaten and scourged, so that by His scourging — by His stripes — you are healed! (Isaiah 53:5) Since He has already suffered the sickness on your behalf, why should you suffer it today?

So my friend, if you are sick, know that God did not give you the disease. Read every healing miracle that Jesus did in the Gospels and see how Jesus is the Lord who heals you. (Exodus 15:26) Hear His gracious words, "I am willing, be healed," and know that they are as much for you today as they were for the leper!

By Jesus' Stripes You Are Healed

You know, one of the biggest outcries against Mel Gibson's movie, *The Passion Of The Christ*, was that it was too violent, especially the part where Jesus was scourged.

Let me tell you this: It was not violent enough! The Bible says that at the cross, Jesus' visage was marred beyond that of any man. (Isaiah 52:14) In the movie, even after all the beatings, the actor James Caviezel, who played Jesus, still looked quite handsome.

But the reality is that when Jesus hung on the cross, He had "no form or comeliness... there is no beauty that we should desire Him". (Isaiah 53:2) He was beaten to a pulp until His face looked like jelly hanging out!

In the movie, when they scourged Him, only a small portion of His bones was exposed, so it was still quite tidy. But the messianic psalms say, "The plowers plowed on my back; they made their furrows long" (Psalm 129:3), and "I can count all My bones. They look and stare at Me". (Psalm 22:17) All His bones were exposed!

My friend, He was thinking of you when the soldiers tied Him to the scourging post. As they raised their whips, He said, "Let it all come on Me!"

But what came on Him was not just the whip stripping the flesh off His bare back, but your sicknesses and diseases. Each time He was whipped, every form of sickness and disease, including arthritis, cancer, diabetes, bird flu and dengue fever, came upon Him. "The chastisement for our peace was upon Him, and by His stripes we are healed."

Today, healing is your right because Jesus has paid the price for your healing. So if the devil says, "You cannot be healed," just declare, "Jesus has paid for my healing. Disease has no right to be in my body. I am healed in Jesus' name!"

Every curse of sickness that was supposed to fall on you fell on Jesus instead. He bore every one of those stripes, so that you can walk in divine health all the days of your life. The price has been paid so that you can rise up and get out of your bed of affliction!

33Who shall bring a charge against God's elect? It is God who justifies.

Romans 8:33

God Is Not Judging You

Some people see God as a judge who has exacting demands on man. When they fall short or when things go wrong in their lives, they think that God is judging them.

My friend, the truth is that if you are a believer, God does not bring any charge against you. Instead, He justifies you because of the blood of His Son. In fact, God's Word goes on to say that the One who has the right to condemn you, chose instead to die for you and is risen at the Father's right hand to be your righteousness! (Romans 8:34)

But what the devil tries to do is to get you to believe that God watches you with a critical eye and punishes you when you do wrong. He has deceived many sincere Christians into believing that if they have done something wrong, sickness or some other evil thing has a right to come upon them and their families. And when these things happen, he convinces them that they are suffering God's judgment because of their wrongdoings. In the meantime, these sincere Christians struggle with condemnation because they think that they are the cause of their problems.

Nothing could be further from the truth. Ever since the cross, where Jesus was judged in your place for every one of your wrong actions, thoughts and words, God no longer judges you, His child. You need not accept condemnation or evil things happening to you because Jesus took all your punishment at the cross.

So when you start to feel condemned for your actions or when you experience negative circumstances, say, "It is written: It is God who justifies me. I am completely forgiven and made righteous before Him. I refuse to accept any condemnation and I reject every symptom of the curse that I am seeing in my circumstances!"

Then, simply stand on the truth of God's Word, and watch Him deliver and bless you!

God Is Your Strength

When you say, "I can manage this problem by myself, Lord," God says, "Okay, you do it then." But when you say, "Help me, Lord! I need You. I cannot do this on my own," God says, "Good, I have been waiting for you to say that. You cannot, but I can. Now, watch Me!" That is how God is — He loves it when you depend on Him.

You see, when you think that you are strong and don't need God, He cannot help you. But when you need Him and look to Him, He will not leave you weak and helpless. He comes and becomes the strength of your life. He becomes the breakthrough that you need.

A church member with a smoking habit came to me one day and said, "Pastor Prince, please pray that God will help me. I want to stop my smoking habit."

I told him simply, "You cannot, but God can."

He replied, "Yes, I know that I can't. But with God's help, I will discipline myself and try my best to quit the habit."

I told him, "No, you cannot, but God can." I repeated this to him a few times until he realized that it was not his self-discipline or willpower that would help him overcome his smoking habit, but the power of God. He finally understood that true deliverance from this destructive habit would not come by his own strength, but by "[being] strong in the Lord and in the power of **His** might".

When I saw him again a few weeks later, he said, "Pastor Prince, since that day, I didn't even try to stop myself from smoking. But each time I lit up, I told God, 'I cannot, but You can.' Then one day, the craving was gone! Jesus has completely delivered me from my bondage to nicotine!" This man experienced true deliverance, not just an outward form of discipline and willpower.

So when you say, "**I** can do something about it," you are still relying on your human strength. But when you say to God, "I cannot, but **You** can," you have just tapped into the real source of your strength — Jesus. And as you rest in His strength, you will see His power manifesting in your life!

God Gives You Undeserved Preferential Treatment

When you fly first class in an airplane, the cabin crew gives you first-class treatment. They ask you, "Is everything okay with you, sir?" They ask you what magazines you want to read. They give you a blanket if you are cold. They give you the best kinds of food. They give you preferential treatment compared to those traveling in economy class.

The grace of God is defined as "undeserved, unearned and unmerited favor". And one of the definitions for favor is "preferential treatment"! Today, God wants you to know that you have His favor on you. He wants you to know that He gives you preferential treatment which you do not deserve. And He wants you to depend on and take full advantage of it in your life.

God also wants you to know that His favor in your life can be increased. You can experience more of His favor from day to day. How? The Bible tells us in 2 Peter 1:2 that

God's grace (or favor) is multiplied to us "in the knowledge of God and of Jesus our Lord". The more you behold Jesus and His love for you, the more you believe and confess that God's favor is on you, the more you will see His favor work for you.

So if you are a doctor, you will find patients favoring you and you will have more patients than you can handle. If you are a businessman, you will find people just wanting to do business with you because they like you and feel good about you. Then, you will have more business than you can handle and you will need to plan for expansion!

When the favor of God shines on your church, you will find its premises too small for the people who queue up week after week to attend the services! So when people wonder and ask, "What is happening here?" you can tell them, "It is the favor of God multiplied all over us!" And it is all undeserved, unearned and unmerited!

13

28For she said, "If only I may touch His clothes, I shall be made well." 29Immediately the fountain of her blood was dried up, and she felt in her body that she was healed of the affliction.

Mark 5:28–29

Believing Is Receiving

You have heard people of the world say, "I will believe it only when I see it." Generally, that is the way the world thinks. But God's ways are not like the ways of the world. The world says, "If I can't feel it or see it, I cannot believe the miracle is here." God says, "If you believe it before you feel it or see it, you will see your miracle."

Believing first before seeing the evidence of what we are believing for is called faith. Faith is like a spark and Jesus is the dynamite powder.

In the story of the healing of the woman with the issue of blood, there were many people who touched Jesus (Mark 5:31), but nothing happened to them. They didn't touch Him in faith. But when the woman who had been bleeding for 12 years came to Him and touched Him in faith, He felt power leave His body (Mark 5:30), and it sparked off an explosion of healing in the woman's body!

Hearing about how good, kind and loving Jesus was fired her faith to believe that He could and would heal her. So convinced was she (even when the condition in her body was still evident) that she said, "If only I may touch His clothes, I shall be made well." Did she experience her healing first before she believed? No, she believed first in Jesus' goodness and power, acted in faith and only then felt the healing in her body.

In the same way, God wants you to believe in His goodness and love toward you. He wants you to know how willing He is to act on your behalf to bless you, and how, with Christ, He will freely give you every good thing. (Romans 8:32)

He wants you to declare by faith that all is and shall be well with you, and to expect to see just that. And then, no matter how long you have had the problem, no matter how bad the experts say it is, an explosion of healing and restoration will take place, and you will receive what you are believing for!

The Power Of Your Words

Most people, when they desperately want something, will say things like, "I am dying for that piece of cake!" Few will say, "I am living for that piece of cake!"

What is worse is that we are quick to mention death when things go wrong. We Singaporeans are quick to say things like, "Die lah! Die lah!" at the drop of a hat. Nobody says, "Live lah! Live lah!"

Yet, the truth is that every word you speak has power — to build or destroy hopes and dreams, to restore or cause loss, to heal or break the spirit, to bring delight or despair, to bless or curse — for God's Word says that death and life are in the power of the tongue.

So stop lining your words up with the negative circumstances. Instead, start lining your words up with God's Word and release the power of His Word to work for you.

For example, instead of speaking lack and poverty, say, "God's Word tells me that the good things are already here. I therefore pronounce my life blessed. I pronounce my life successful. I pronounce my life great. Darkness and gloom, poverty and sickness, defeat and depression, will not be in my life!"

Instead of speaking sickness and death, say, "I will live long. I will not die young. Jesus died young for me so that I can live long for Him. I am the righteousness of God in Christ and God's Word declares that no evil befalls the righteous. So no evil will come on me now and in the future!"

Instead of speaking fear over your children, say, "God's Word declares that the seed of the righteous shall be delivered. Therefore, my children are delivered from every curse, every power of darkness and every evil. In the name of Jesus, I call forth a great, bright and blessed future for my children!"

God wants you to have a life filled with good days and an abundance of every good thing. So say, "In the name of Jesus, I command blessings, favor, health, provision, protection, dominion and power to fill my life!"

¹²But when Jesus saw her, He called her to Him and said to her, "Woman, you are loosed from your infirmity."

Luke 13:12

Prayers That Proclaim

When you have a need, do you pray or do you plead? Do you begin your prayers with words like, "Please God, please! God, I beg You to have mercy!"

Prayers that plead and beg imply that your heavenly Father is not willing to do it. Yet, He is far more gracious and willing to give to you than you are willing to ask, think or imagine. (Ephesians 3:20) He desires above all things that you prosper and be in health, even as your soul prospers. (3 John 1:2)

In fact, long before you have a need, God has already met that need. Long before you knew you needed a Savior, He sent His Son to be your Savior. This is your God! He is a good God. So when you beg Him for something, you are actually saying that He is reluctant to give and needs to be persuaded strongly before He will move. Yet, He is not like that.

Jesus knew the heart of the Father. When He saw the woman bound with a spirit of infirmity, He did not pray, "Oh Father! She has been suffering for 18 long years! I beseech You, Father, have mercy on her. Please, please heal her!" No, when Jesus saw her, He immediately proclaimed, "Woman, you are loosed from your infirmity," because He knew the heart of the Father. He knew that the Father wanted her delivered from her crippling condition.

At the end of a church service, I don't stand and pray, "Oh God, please bless Your people. Oh God, do keep them. Oh God, be ever so gracious to them!" Instead, I proclaim, "The Lord bless you. The Lord keep you. The Lord make His face shine on you and be gracious to you!"

Beloved, when you pray, proclaim your healing, protection and provision because your Father's heart overflows with love for you. And when you declare it, He sanctions it. When you declare it, He establishes it!

20... that He may send Jesus Christ, who was preached to you before, 21whom heaven must receive until the times of restoration of all things...

Acts 3:20–21

Claim Your Restoration!

As a believer, you have a right to expect restoration of the things that the devil has stolen from you. It may be your health, marriage or finances, but payback time is definitely coming!

Acts 3:20–21 tells us that before Jesus comes back for His church, we will experience "the times of restoration of all things". What a hope that gives us, knowing that God will restore to us all things before Jesus returns!

My friend, if the devil is attacking you in any area, tell God, "Father, I will not allow the devil to rob me of my health, marriage, children or finances. These blessings are blood-bought and paid for by Your Son!" Claim your restoration in Christ and heaven will hear you.

There will be such times of restoration of all things to the body of Christ that His people will only get better, stronger, healthier, and more successful and glorious! When God restores, even under the old covenant, His people always received much more than what they had

originally lost, in terms of quality and/or quantity. How much more will our restoration be under the new covenant because of the shed blood of the Lamb of God!

A divorcee with a teenage son came to our church and accepted the Lord in May 2003. She began to pray for the restoration of her marriage and the reunion of her family. She knew that the chances of this happening were close to zero since she had not met nor spoken with her ex-husband since their divorce 10 years ago. She did not even know if he had remarried. But God caused their paths to cross at a wedding at the end of 2003. Today, their relationship is healed, and together with their son, they worship as a family in church.

Even though what happened for that sister may not happen for every divorced person (God can give you a better spouse and marriage), I believe that God wants you to know that your times of restoration are here. Heaven is waiting to hear you stake your claim for restoration!

The Gift Of No Condemnation

When Jesus was on earth, a woman caught in the act of adultery was brought before Him by the scribes and Pharisees, the religious mafia of His day. They tried to trap Him by posing a question that was difficult to answer: "Now Moses, in the law, commanded us that such should be stoned. But what do You say?" (John 8:5)

Jesus answered, "He who is without sin among you, let him throw a stone at her first." (John 8:7) The scribes and Pharisees began to leave one by one till none of them were left.

The people in the crowd who wanted to condemn the woman **could not**. But Jesus, the only one in the crowd who truly had the power to condemn her, **would not**. He then asked her, "Woman... Has no one condemned you?" (John 8:10)

He spoke such words of grace to her because He loved her. Also, by asking her the question, He was giving her a chance to speak words of no condemnation to herself — "No one [condemns me], Lord." (John 8:11)

Jesus not only spoke words of grace to her, He also gave her the gift of no condemnation — "Neither do I condemn you; go and sin no more". It was when she received the gift of no condemnation that she had the power to "go and sin no more".

Today, you have the gift of no condemnation because the Son of God was condemned for all your sins. (Romans 8:1) Today, God cannot condemn you when you sin because He is faithful and just to what His Son has done.

So if the devil tries to convince you that God is angry with you when you blow it, just say, "God **does not** condemn me today because He has already condemned Jesus at the cross 2,000 years ago!"

Unfortunately, we still hear people saying, "Go and sin no more **first**, then I won't condemn you." Maybe you have been saying this to yourself too. But God says, "I don't condemn you. Go and sin no more." He gives you the gift of no condemnation, so that you have the strength to go and sin no more!

²So Ruth the Moabitess said to Naomi, "Please let me go to the field, and glean heads of grain after him in whose sight I may find favor." And she said to her, "Go, my daughter."

Ruth 2:2

Beat The Odds With The Favor Of God

Do you look at yourself and see only lack in the natural? Do you say, "I don't have a good education", "I am poor", "I am too old" or "I am a divorcee"? I have good news for you. As a blood-bought believer and child of God, you have the supernatural favor of God!

In the Bible, Ruth was a poor Moabite widow who went with her mother-in-law to live in Bethlehem, a Jewish town where the inhabitants considered Moabites outcasts. But she did not wallow in self-pity and moan about being a poor widow of the wrong race in the wrong place. Instead, she believed that God would favor her and she declared, "I will find favor in the field that I glean from."

In the natural, Ruth had everything going against her. But because she trusted in the favor of God, she not only became the wife of Bethlehem's richest man when Boaz married her, she also became the great-grandmother of David and had her name included in the genealogy of Jesus Christ even though she was not a Jewess! That is what God's supernatural favor did for her. That is the kind of blessing God's supernatural favor can give you.

A church member shared how, due to unforeseen circumstances, she was late for a job interview. But she confessed God's favor on herself before the interview and miraculously, the interviewers shortlisted her for a second interview.

There were about 40 other applicants with the right experience. And though she lacked the relevant experience, by the favor of God, she got the job which came with better pay and a car allowance that fully subsidized her car loan. Her new company was even willing to pay for her petrol and cell phone expenses — all because she believed and confessed that she had the favor of God!

Do not look at what you do not have in the natural and see lack. Trust in the favor of God and you will see blessings which your natural abilities cannot bring!

[11]So shall My word be that goes forth from My mouth; it shall not return to Me void, but it shall accomplish what I please, and it shall prosper in the thing for which I sent it.

Isaiah 55:11

God's Word Is Out To Bless You

In the early church, whenever the Word of God was preached, there were miracles of salvation, healings, and other signs and wonders. The demon-possessed were set free. The paralyzed jumped up and walked. People received their loved ones back from the dead.

I remember saying in one of our church services that there was an anointing for couples, who were told that they could not conceive in the natural, to receive the children they had been believing God for. As the word went forth, many couples received their miracle in that service.

One of the ladies who received was serving that day as an usher. She and her husband had been believing God for a child for a few years. A few months after that service, she realized that she was pregnant — with twins! God's anointing is always greater than our asking.

I believe with all of my heart that we are truly coming to the place where as the Word of God goes forth, it produces the very effect that the Word promises. So if the Word on healing goes forth, know that healing is already exploding in your body. Your miracle has already happened.

Very often, as you are reading the Word on your own or listening to anointed preaching of the Word, you will feel God's peace and joy, and feel faith springing up in your heart. As the Word goes forth and you find that you are strengthened to receive your miracle, that is the time to say, "Lord, I receive my healing right now." That is the time to say, "I receive Your restoration for my marriage." That is the time to say, "I receive Your breakthrough for my finances."

You don't have to wait until a church leader or friend prays for you. Every time your faith is strengthened as you hear the Word, release it through your mouth to receive your miracle, for God's Word is out to bless you!

13... And when I see the blood, I will pass over you; and the plague shall not be on you to destroy you when I strike the land of Egypt.

Exodus 12:13

The Blood Of Jesus Protects

For 400 years, the children of Israel were slaves in Egypt. Life for them was one of hard labor, pain, loss and even death. When Moses their deliverer came, what soon followed was one plague after another on the Egyptians. But none of the plagues caused Pharaoh to release the Israelites until they put the blood on their doorposts. What nine plagues could not do, the blood did! The Israelites were finally set free because of the blood.

Are you under any kind of bondage? Are your loved ones held captive by the destroyer who is bent on destroying them? Plead the blood of the Lamb of God over all that is yours and your family's. When nothing else seems to work, His blood always works!

When I was a teenager doing a stint as a relief teacher in a primary school, one of the girls in my class was absent from school one day. I didn't think too much about her absence until I returned home that afternoon. As I was praying, I was prompted by the Holy Spirit to pray

for her protection and to cover her with the precious blood of Jesus.

It was revealed later on that she had been abducted by a notorious serial killer who had murdered a number of young children. My pupil recounted how she had been tied up and offered to the "deities" the killer had in his flat. Miraculously, he released her when the evil spirits found her to be an unsuitable offering.

Why was this pupil released unharmed? I believe that she was presented to the deities on the same afternoon that I pleaded the blood of Jesus over her. Of course, the evil spirits did not want her because the Most High God would not allow them to have her. God was protecting her. She was set free because of the blood of Jesus!

You see, when you plead the blood of Jesus, the destroyer cannot come near. When he sees the blood, he must respect the blood. He cannot touch what is covered by the blood. The blood of Jesus truly protects and sets you free!

come to Jesus first not last

⁸And he said, "Lord God, how shall I know that I will inherit it?" ⁹So He said to him, "Bring Me a three-year-old heifer, a three-year-old female goat, a three-year-old ram, a turtledove, and a young pigeon."

Genesis 15:8–9

Guaranteed By Covenant

Are you discouraged because a breakthrough that you have been praying for has yet to manifest? Maybe it has been days or even weeks and you are asking, "How will I know that I will get it?" Abraham faced the same situation and asked God the same question. And God answered, "Bring Me a three-year-old heifer, a three-year-old female goat, a three-year-old ram, a turtledove, and a young pigeon." What a strange answer!

But if you read on (Genesis 15:10–21), you will realize that God took Abraham's question very seriously, and went on to show him just how serious He was about being his provider, protector and blesser. God was so serious that He was willing to bind Himself to a **covenant**.

What is a covenant? It is like a contract. Yet, it is more than a contract. A contract is binding only for a period of time, like five years or seven years, or until certain terms are fulfilled. But a covenant is perpetual. It is permanent. The only way out is through death. That is why marriage is a covenant, not a contract. It is permanent — "Till death do us part".

In Bible times, when you cut a covenant with someone, you bring an animal, usually a ram or goat, and kill it by cutting it in two. Next, you will face your covenant partner and walk toward each other between the two pieces of the animal, passing each other in the center.

What all this means is that both parties are obligated to protect and provide for each other. Whatever belongs to you is your partner's and whatever belongs to your partner is yours. Of course, the one who benefits is the lesser or poorer party.

Today, God is in covenant with us. We are the lesser, poorer party. We have nothing to offer God. But God, the richest and most powerful being in the universe, has everything to offer us!

My friend, God has bound Himself to a covenant, an iron-clad guarantee of His blessings and provision in your life, and it is all for your benefit. The breakthrough you are waiting for is guaranteed by covenant!

A Sleeping Partner Who Benefits

In business, sleeping or silent partners don't work but still take home huge profits. They are like the wife of the boxing champion. He gets badly beaten up to win the prize money. But when he gets home, his wife takes it from him and says, "Thank you very much, darling!"

Do you know that in your covenant with God, you are like the boxer's wife or the sleeping partner?

When Abraham asked God how he would know for sure that he would inherit the land that God had promised him, God made a covenant with him. (Genesis 15:8–21) But instead of cutting the covenant with Abraham by walking in between the animal pieces with him, God put Abraham into a deep sleep and cut the covenant with Jesus instead.

Jesus, the light of the world, appeared as the pillar of fire and cut the covenant with God the Father who appeared as the pillar of cloud. In other words, Jesus took Abraham's place. He was perfect Man representing Abraham when He cut the covenant with His Father.

By substituting Abraham with Jesus, God was being gracious because if Abraham had done it, he would also have been responsible for keeping the covenant. And Abraham, being a mere man, would fail. But God the Son can never fail! Abraham's blessings were therefore guaranteed because they did not depend on his performance but **Jesus'** performance. Abraham was literally a sleeping partner, a beneficiary of the covenant.

Today, God has also made a covenant with you, called the new covenant. And like Abraham, you are a sleeping partner because the new covenant was also cut between God the Father and God the Son at Calvary. You are simply a beneficiary of the new covenant. You enjoy all its benefits without having to work at keeping it. Jesus, your representative, has already fulfilled all the conditions on your behalf. And because His obedience is perfect and His work is perfectly finished, the covenant blessings for you are guaranteed!

My friend, there is nothing left for you to do, but everything for you to believe. Don't try to work for your covenant blessings. Rest in the Son's finished work and receive them by faith!

27... *"Rejoice, O barren, you who do not bear! Break forth and shout, you who are not in labor...*

Galatians 4:27

Rejoice, O Barren!

Barrenness. What a painful and frustrating condition. Yet, in Isaiah 54, God's Word to those who are experiencing barrenness is to rejoice — "Sing O barren"!

Why? Because in the previous chapter, it tells us that the chastisement for our peace fell upon Jesus. (Isaiah 53:5) The word "peace" here in Hebrew means completeness, soundness, health, safety and provision. In other words, all these benefits are yours today because Jesus has already been punished at the cross for your peace. That is why you can start rejoicing.

So God wants you right now, in whatever area you are barren, to start rejoicing as if the fruit or yield you want to see has already come. He wants you to start thinking, speaking and acting as if the barrenness is no more.

If you are financially barren, start planning for what you would do when your finances increase. I am not saying that you go out and spend recklessly, but start making plans for increase. The time to do this is when you are still in what your natural eyes see as a barren stage.

You may say, "Pastor Prince, you don't understand, the banks are chasing me!"

God says, "Rejoice because you are well provided for in Christ." In Christ, you are already blessed with every spiritual blessing, including financial provision. (Ephesians 1:3) "For you know the grace of our Lord Jesus Christ, that though He was rich, yet for your sakes He became poor, that you through His poverty might become rich." (2 Corinthians 8:9)

If you are sick, start planning to do what you have not been able to do. Don't rejoice only when the healing manifests and the pain is no more. Rejoice now in your healing because Jesus has already borne your diseases and carried your pains, and by His stripes you have already been healed. (Isaiah 53:4–5)

Whatever barren situation you are in, rejoice and tell God, "Father, because of the sacrifice of Your Son, I am blessed with all spiritual blessings in heavenly places in Christ. You have already given me everything. So I am going to act like it is so and rejoice!"

Surely!

While waiting for the manifestation of their healing, some people find it hard to believe that Jesus really took their sicknesses and pains, just as He took their sin and shame. If you are one of them, don't feel condemned. Your Father in heaven understands. That is why He put the word "surely" there when He said, "**Surely**, My Son has borne your sicknesses and carried your pains."

Once, my daughter Jessica was crying all night because she was not feeling well. She had been sick for a few days. In my study, I took out my Bible and the Lord led me to Isaiah 53:4 where it says, "Surely He has borne…" Now, I know the original Hebrew here and it says, "Surely He has borne our sicknesses and carried our pains." So I said, "Surely, He has borne Jessica's sickness…"

But it was like the verse was just not real to me. Her cries seemed more real. Then, all of a sudden, the Holy Spirit opened my eyes to a word in the verse that really revolutionized the way I saw the whole passage.

Notice the first word in the verse? It says, "Surely…" Surely, He has borne our sicknesses and carried our pains. Now, look at the next verse: "He was wounded for our transgressions…" Every Christian knows and believes that Jesus was wounded for our sins, yet the word "surely" is not put here but in the earlier verse. I think God knew that we would find it hard to believe that Jesus also bore our sicknesses and carried our pains, so He put the word "surely" there to help us believe!

When I saw that, I put my Bible on the floor, stood on it and said, "Father, you know I don't mean any irreverence, but I am standing on Your Word. **Surely**, Jesus bore Jessica's sickness and carried her pain! I don't care if I can still hear her crying. **Surely**, Your Son, Your beloved Son, bore her sickness and carried her pain! Hallelujah!" That night, the breakthrough came. That night, little Jessica was healed.

Are you or your loved ones suffering some sickness or pain right now?

Surely our Lord Jesus has borne your sicknesses and carried your pains. And as you believe this truth, **surely**, your healing and breakthrough will come!

See The Favor Of God Multiplied In Your Life

If you would like to walk in a greater measure of God's favor, 2 Peter 1:2 says that grace, which is the undeserved favor of God, and peace, can be multiplied to you. Peace is the word "shalom" in Hebrew. Its definition includes wholeness, health, safety and provision. So when you walk in divine favor and peace, you will walk in blessings in every area of your life!

But how do the undeserved favor and shalom of God increase in your life?

It is not by your laboring or toiling to earn it. The Bible says that it comes as your knowledge of Jesus and His finished work increases. It comes as you learn more about and believe that through Jesus' one sacrifice at the cross, God removed all your sins, gave you His righteousness as a gift and put you in Christ to enjoy everything Jesus has. God's favor is multiplied in your life when you simply believe that the favor of God that is on Christ is also on you because of what Jesus' work at the cross has accomplished.

Today, you don't have to struggle for favor. Just release it by speaking forth God's Word in faith. On your way to work, say, "God's favor surrounds me as with a shield." (Psalm 5:12) As you continue to speak God's favor over your life out of a revelation of Jesus' finished work, you will see more of it being released.

When I first entered the workforce, I began to declare the favor of God in my job. Every time I was given a new assignment, I proclaimed that the divine favor of God was on me. The company began to prosper and I was blessed financially. By the time I left the company to serve God full-time, my income had increased so that I was in the top 15 per cent of earners in my age group in Singapore.

Today, in your workplace or at home, begin to declare the favor of God by faith. Expect to receive preferential treatment wherever you are. Say, "I am surrounded with the favor of God because of Jesus' finished work. I have favor before God and man!" And see God's favor work for you!

Confessing Your Righteousness Pleases God

Every time you confess, "I am the righteousness of God in Christ", God the Father is pleased. When you confess that you are the righteousness of God in Christ, it reminds Him of what His Son has done for you to become righteous.

Also, by making you righteous, God is showing Himself righteous — "to demonstrate at the present time His righteousness, that He might be just and the justifier of the one who has faith in Jesus". (Romans 3:26)

Each time Jesus hears you confess, "I am the righteousness of God in Christ," it brings much pleasure to His heart too, because you are laying hold of what He suffered and died to give you.

The Holy Spirit, who now indwells you to convict you of righteousness (John 16:10), also rejoices when you confess, "I am the righteousness of God in Christ." He is pleased when you flow with Him.

The delight of the Godhead is not the only thing you gain when you declare, "I am the righteousness of God in Christ." The Bible tells us that when you "seek first the kingdom of God and **His righteousness**... all these things shall be added to you". (Matthew 6:33)

Whether it is food, clothing or other necessities in life, "all these things" will be added to you. They will not just be given to you, but **added** to you as your inheritance when you seek first His righteousness.

You don't need to use your faith for every single need in life. You just need to use your faith for one thing — to believe that you are the righteousness of God in Christ, and it will cause all the blessings you seek to come after you and overtake you!

Call It Forth!

"Pastor Prince, I feel the pain in my body. How can I go around saying that Christ has redeemed me from this sickness? How can I say that by His stripes I am healed?"

Well, God's way is to call those things that are not as though they are. And because you are made in God's image, you can also call those things that are not as though they are!

When God wanted to make Abraham a father of many nations, what did He do? He changed the way Abraham talked. At that time, Abraham did not even have a single child from Sarah because she was barren. So how could he become a father of many nations?

God changed the way he talked. How? By changing his name from Abram to Abraham, which means "father of many nations". (Genesis 17:5)

Just imagine: From then on, every time he met someone, he would say, "Hi, my name is Father Of Many Nations." Every time dinner was ready, Sarah would call out to Abraham, "Darling... Father Of Many Nations... dinner is ready! Father Of Many Nations..." You can just hear their neighbors saying, "They want a child so much they have gone mad!" But God changed the way Abraham talked so that he called forth what God saw him already blessed with.

You know, when Jesus saw the man with a withered hand, He didn't say, "My goodness! It is so withered!" He said, "Stretch out your hand!" (Matthew 12:13) He called forth what He wanted. He looked at the paralytic and said, "Rise, take up your bed and go home!" (Matthew 9:6) He didn't see the way it was in the natural. He saw the way God meant it to be and He called it forth.

Genesis 1 tells us that in the beginning, there was darkness over the face of the whole earth. God saw the darkness and He said, "Light be!" And light was. God called forth what He wanted and it became so! If it had been me or you, we would probably have said, "Whoa! It is so dark!"

My friend, despite the pain, call forth your healing. It is pointless to state the obvious. So change the way you talk. See the way God meant it to be, and start calling forth your healing and wholeness!

[24]Therefore I say to you, whatever things you ask when you pray,
believe that you receive them, and you will have them.

Mark 11:24

You Already Are, You Already Have

*G*od's Word tells us that we can have what we ask for in prayer — by simply believing that we already have it! As you are praying, know that you already have your answer or breakthrough — "**believe** that you **receive** them". The Bible also tells us that we already have whatever we are praying for because we are already blessed with every spiritual blessing in heavenly places in Christ. (Ephesians 1:3)

And you are in Christ the moment you received Him as your Savior. So when you pray, you are actually releasing your faith to lay hold of what you already have in Christ. And as you keep saying that you already have it (Mark 11:23), you **will** see the manifestation of it in the natural realm.

In one of our church camps, a church member shared about the back problem she had had for 15 years as a result of a fall from her rooftop. She needed an operation to help stop the shooting pains in her spine. She had also been taking anti-stress pills for five years.

After coming to church, she realized that she had already received her healing through the finished work of Christ. Refusing the operation and even the pills, she would rebuke the pain which kept coming back, saying, "In Jesus, I believe I am healed. I am not trying or going to be healed. I am already healed. I have a brand new backbone for I am in Christ. As Christ is, so am I in this world." It was not very long before this sister saw the manifestation of her healing.

Sometimes, the symptoms of a sickness or lack may return and you think that you still have not received your blessing. That is the time to release your faith and declare that you already have it. You are not confessing to get it. You are confessing because you already have it in Christ!

My friend, the Bible tells us that Christ is in us. (Colossians 1:27) This means that right now, your healing, wellness, family's well-being and everything your heart desires are in you. So say, "I have everything I need in Christ right now!"

7In Him we have redemption through His blood, the forgiveness of sins, according to the riches of His grace

Ephesians 1:7

[handwritten: Self control can become prideful pride is sin.]

Be Christ-Conscious

Have you ever woken up in the morning and said, "Today, I will not sin." And as you leave your house, you say, "I must be careful not to fall into sin today. I don't want to sin. I will not sin!" My friend, when you do this, you are no longer Christ-conscious but sin-conscious, even though you have not sinned yet.

Men, have you ever caught yourself thinking, "I don't want to look at any woman in case I lust"? You are being sin-conscious when you think like that. And sooner or later, you will lust in your heart. You may not sin outwardly, but you will sin inwardly.

Have you also tried confessing every sin? I have! As a teenager, when a bad thought came, I would quickly say, "I'm sorry, Lord. Forgive me for this thought in Jesus' name." Then, another thought would come and I would quickly say, "Forgive me, Lord, for that thought in Jesus' name." Then, if I happen to doubt His forgiveness, I would confess my unbelief and ask for forgiveness: "Forgive me, Lord, for doubting You." Before I knew it, I was oppressed in my mind and so sin-conscious instead of Christ-conscious!

My friend, when you fall into sin, God wants you to be Christ-conscious. This means that when you have missed it, God wants you to be conscious that in Christ, you have forgiveness of sins through His blood. God wants you to be conscious that Christ was wounded and bruised for your sins, and that the chastisement for your peace was upon Him. (Isaiah 53:5)

When you are Christ-conscious, you will have peace with God through our Lord Jesus Christ. (Romans 5:1) You will know that you are the righteousness of God in Christ because He who knew no sin was made sin for you. (2 Corinthians 5:21) He took your sin and now you have His righteousness.

So when you fall, don't be conscious of your failure and feel bad or condemned. Instead, be conscious of who you are in Christ, pick yourself up, dust yourself off and continue your walk with God!

30

"Blessed are those whose lawless deeds are forgiven, and whose sins are covered; ⁸blessed is the man to whom the Lord shall not impute sin."

Romans 4:7–8

God Hears Your Prayers

Some people think that if they were more "right" with God, then He would hear their prayers. For example, they sometimes believe that if they had not quarreled with their wives or had those bad thoughts earlier in the day, then God would answer their prayers.

God is not like that. He wants you to know beyond any doubt that you can always come to His throne of grace with boldness and have every confidence that you **will** receive His mercy and grace. (Hebrews 4:16) You see, because of Jesus' finished work on the cross, you are already right with God. You don't need to do anything to make yourself more right with God.

In fact, by faith in Jesus, you have received the righteousness of God Himself! (2 Corinthians 5:21) And no matter how many mistakes you make, you will never lose that righteousness because in the first place, God gave it to you **apart** from your works. (Romans 4:5–6) In other words, God did not impute righteousness to you because you were good, but because you believed in Jesus.

Because of what Jesus has done for you at the cross, all your sins — past, present and future — are forgiven. God will by no means ever remember your sins or count them against you! (Hebrews 8:12, 10:17)

My friend, because Jesus has been punished for your sins, today, God is not counting your sins against you. This means that your sins won't stop Him from hearing and responding to your prayers. So you can always run into His presence knowing that you can boldly stand in and enjoy His presence and His love.

When you know this truth, it is going to set you free in your relationship with God. You can talk to Him without fear or any sense of condemnation. You can practice His presence and trust that He always hears you. Should something happen at home or at work, you don't always have to call for your church leaders — you pray and God hears you!

Beloved, you are righteous in Christ and God hears your prayers — all because of Jesus!

26... "Take, eat; this is My body."
Matthew 26:26

Power From Jesus' Body To Yours

Can you imagine the Lord sick, nursing a cold or fever while He walked on earth? No, our Lord Jesus was never sick! He was vibrant, full of life and full of health. When He told His disciples, "Take, eat; this is My body", they could practically visualize what it meant because they had lived and walked with this Man. They had seen people without hands or feet made whole when they touched His body. (Matthew 15:30–31)

Even His clothes were soaked with His health! A woman who had a bleeding condition for 12 years — no doctor could cure her — was healed immediately when she touched the hem of His garment. If the hem of His garment was soaked with His health, vibrancy, energy and divine radiance, how much more His body!

You know, some of the most encouraging verses in the Gospels are these: "And as many as touched Him were made well" (Mark 6:56), for "power went out from Him and healed them all". (Luke 6:19) I love those verses! That is our Jesus!

The Bible says that they put sick people along the streets, and Jesus walked around, touched them and healed them. Now, you see movie stars doing this: They run here and there, they slap their fans' hands, but nobody gets healed. But wherever Jesus walked, whoever He touched, He healed. Picture this: A trail of people. Those in front of Jesus are lying down, but those behind Him whom He has touched are leaping with joy and following Him! That is how Jesus healed the sick.

So that night, when He said, "Take, eat; this is My body," as He broke the bread and gave it to His disciples to eat, they knew what it meant. They were probably thinking, "We are going to ingest His health into our bodies! Hallelujah!"

That is what you must believe when you partake of the Holy Communion. It is not just a ritual or symbolic act. No, you must believe that He is the true bread from heaven who took your cancer, diabetes and heart disease, so that you can have His supernatural health! And when you eat of His broken body with this revelation, you will have life in abundance and the health of the Lord!